First World War
and Army of Occupation
War Diary
France, Belgium and Germany

51 DIVISION
Divisional Troops
260 Brigade Royal Field Artillery
22 October 1915 - 28 February 1917

WO95/2854/6

The Naval & Military Press Ltd
www.nmarchive.com
Published in association with The National Archives

Published by

The Naval & Military Press Ltd

Unit 10 Ridgewood Industrial Park,

Uckfield, East Sussex,

TN22 5QE England

Tel: +44 (0) 1825 749494

www.naval-military-press.com

www.nmarchive.com

This diary has been reprinted in facsimile from the original. Any imperfections are inevitably reproduced and the quality may fall short of modern type and cartographic standards.

© **Crown Copyright**
Images reproduced by permission of The National Archives, London, England, 2015.

Contents

Document type	Place/Title	Date From	Date To
Heading	WO95/2854/6 260 Brig. Royal Field Artillery 1915 Oct-1917 Feb		
Heading	51st Division 260 (Lowland) Bde RFA. Oct 1915-Feb 1917 Broken H.P		
Heading	1/1 High Bde RFA Feb Vol IX		
Heading	1/2 High Bde RFA Feb Vol X		
War Diary		22/10/1915	29/02/1916
Heading	No Diaries For March & April 1916		
War Diary	In The Field	01/05/1916	30/06/1916
Heading	War Diary of 260th Brigade R.F.A. Shown As 258 May & June from 1st July 1916 to 31st July 1916 (Volume) Vol 10		
War Diary		02/07/1916	30/07/1916
Heading	51st Divisional Artillery. 260th Brigade Royal Field Artillery August 1916		
War Diary	The Field	01/08/1916	30/09/1916
Miscellaneous	Headquarters. 51st Divl Arty.	03/08/1916	03/08/1916
Heading	War Diary of 260th (Lowland) Brigade, R.F.A. for September 1916 Vol 12		
Heading	War Diary of 260th (Lowland) Brigade R.F.A. From 1st to 31st October 1916 Vol 13		
War Diary	The Field	01/10/1916	31/10/1916
Heading	War Diary of 260th (Lowland) Brigade, RFA. From 1 November 1916 to 30 November 1916 Vol 14		
War Diary	The Field	01/11/1916	30/11/1916
Heading	War Diary of 260th (Lowland) Brigade R.F.A. from 1st December 1916 to 31 December 1916. Vol 15		
War Diary	The Field	01/12/1916	31/12/1916
Heading	War Diary of 260th (Lowland) Brigade, R.F.A. From 1st January 1917 to 31st January 1917		
War Diary	The Field	01/01/1917	31/01/1917
Heading	War Diary of 260 (Lowland) Brigade R.F.A. From 1st February 1917 to 28th February 1917. both inclusive Vol 17		
War Diary	The Field.	01/02/1917	28/02/1917

WO 95 2854/6

260 BRIG. ROYAL FIELD ARTILLERY

1915 OCT — 1917 FEB

51ST DIVISION

260 (LOWLAND) BDE RFA.
OCT 1915-FEB 1917

BROKEN UP

51

1/1 High Bde R␣Fa
Feb IX
Vol ~~VIII~~

51

1/2 Hist Bde R 7a

Feb

Vol X

October

1/1st Wessex F.A. Bde.

WAR DIARY
or
INTELLIGENCE SUMMARY

Army Form C. 2118

(Erase heading not required.)

Place	Date	Hour	Summary of Events and Information	Remarks and references to Appendices
	1915 Oct 22		The Brigade left Romford Barracks, Colchester for service overseas. The guns were taken at 10 am order to hand over the 15 pr guns & ammunition waggons to the 2nd line.	
	23		Arrived Southampton and left in three boats at night.	
	24		Arrived at Havre and marched to No. 2 camp at Havre on the high ground about there. The Batteries took over the 18 pr guns and waggons and the ammunition blown over the 18 pr waggons before moving into camp.	
	26		Stables and Ammunition Colonnes started drilling at 26/11 camp Harfleur under instructions from the Artillery training branch there until entrained daily owing the Brigade stay at Havre.	

J. Hindley
Lieut. Col.
Commanding 1/1st Wessex and F.A. Bde.

NOVEMBER.

1/1 Highland FA Bde

Army Form C. 2118

WAR DIARY
or
INTELLIGENCE SUMMARY
(Erase heading not required.)

Place	Date	Hour	Summary of Events and Information	Remarks and references to Appendices
	1915 Nov 8th		Medlothian & 1st City of Edinburgh Batteries co-operated with infantry in a Junction battle at Hayling. Infantry having crossed	
	9th		The Brigade entrained to go up North to join the 51st (Highland) Division. Command of Major General J.M. Bannatine Allason Devolved on Brig. General M.J. Wheatley	
	10th		Brigade entrained at Forth, Brigade Headquarters and the Batteries marched to Hawley and Ammunition Column to Hurley where the billets are	
	13th		Batteries and Ammunition Column received their Ammunition Supply	
	14th		Captains Lowe, Blackerley & Philis and Lieutenants Chapin, Frederic & Buchan and 2 Telephonists for battery attached to Batteries of the 1st and 2nd Highland F.A. Brigades and Lieut. Sansom attached to Headquarters 1st Highland F.A. Brigade with 2 Telephonists	
	15th		Lieuts R.G. Maclergan, J.R. Thomson & T. Hinworth who were left behind when the Brigade left England rejoined	

NOVEMBER.

1/1st Lothians & A Bde   Army Form C. 2118.

WAR DIARY
or
INTELLIGENCE SUMMARY
(Erase heading not required.)

Instructions regarding War Diaries and Intelligence Summaries are contained in F. S. Regs., Part II. and the Staff Manual respectively. Title Pages will be prepared in manuscript.

Place	Date	Hour	Summary of Events and Information	Remarks and references to Appendices
	1915 Nov. 10th		Officers who went up the line on 14th Nov returned and Major Mackay Jenkins and Anderson and Lieut Anderson, Scobey and Fawley & 2 Lieutenants went up to the 1st & 2nd Highland Batteries.	
	26th		Officers who went up the line on 19th returned.	
	27th		One section of 2nd Hy.H Battery took over from one section of Fife Battery 2nd Highland Brigade who moved into a new position. One section of Midlothian Battery went into action in an old French position in left of Forfar Battery 2nd Highland Brigade just south of Vitewil.	
	28th		Second section of Midlothian Battery went into action.	
	30th		First section of 1st City of Edinburgh Battery took over from 1st City of Aberdeen Battery who went out to rest. Position just east of Aveluy. Second section of 2nd City of Edinburgh Battery went into action.	

J.H. Anderson Lieut Col
Commanding 1/1st Lothians and A Bde. 15th November

DECEMBER.

Army Form C. 2118.

1/1 Lowland F.A. Bde

WAR DIARY
or
INTELLIGENCE SUMMARY
(Erase heading not required.)

Instructions regarding War Diaries and Intelligence Summaries are contained in F.S. Regs., Part II. and the Staff Manual respectively. Title Pages will be prepared in manuscript.

Place	Date	Hour	Summary of Events and Information	Remarks and references to Appendices
	1915 Decr 1st		The Adjutant attached to Headquarters 1st Highland Brigade. 2nd Lieut Thomson sent to 2nd Bty of Aberdeen 1st Highland Brigade who were short of Officers	
	2nd		Lieut Halford sent to School of Gunnery at Horsham	
	4th		Second section 1st Bty of Edinburgh Battery sent into action. Captain Douglas A.D.C. posted to Veterinary Hospital at Mont Chalet	
	5th		2/Lieut Thomson returned from 1st Highland Brigade	
	7th		Adjutant returned from 1st Highland Brigade	
	9th		Lieut Chyne left on special leave on account of the death of his Father	
	11th		Lieut Jamison went to 1st Highland Brigade as Orderly Officer	
	16th		Colonel attached to 1st Highland Brigade	
	17th		Lieut Michael returned from Horsham	
	19th		Received official intimation of appointment of Lieut Chyne to be A.D.C. and Intelligence officer to G.O.C. R.A. 13th Corps dated 8th Decr. On return of 1st Bty of Edinburgh Battery sent back to waggon lines to allow our Section Officer Church, F. Noble, on for instruction 2nd & 3rd Aberdeen Batteries also changed our Section	

DECEMBER

1/1st Lowland F.A.Bde.

Army Form C. 2118

WAR DIARY
or
INTELLIGENCE SUMMARY

(Erase heading not required.)

Place	Date	Hour	Summary of Events and Information	Remarks and references to Appendices
	1915 Dec 20th		Brigade Headquarters moved to a hut to take over Right Artillery Group from 1/2nd Highland Brigade. Batteries on the group were right & left 2 batty of Ardwin, 1st batty of Edinburgh, 2nd batty of Edinburgh and 2nd batty of Ardwin and 2nd Argyle (Mtn) Battery. 2nd Highland Brigade. The 19th Division in our right. The Midlothian Battery are on the left Artillery Group and in Colonel Bride's 2nd Highland B'de. The 4th Division are on the left of the 51st.	
	21st		Returns of Christmas Batteries sent back and original returns returned. In the afternoon the Group's Trenches were shifted in which all the Batteries of the Brigade took part. The 7. T. C. R.A. 10th Corps complimented the Midlothian Battery on their shooting on this occasion. Colonel visited all Batteries in the Group and the Midlothian Battery in the morning.	
	22nd		Brigade Headquarters had a few shells dropped near it about 4 P.M. our landing outside was. No harm done except broken glass.	[signature] Lt.Col 1/1st Lowland F.A Bde. Commanding 1/1st Lowland F.A Bde.

1875 Wt. W593/826 1,000,000 4/15 J.B.C. & A. A.D.S.S./Forms/C. 2118.

JANUARY 1916   1/1 Lowland F A Brigade

WAR DIARY
or
INTELLIGENCE SUMMARY.

Army Form C. 2118.

Place	Date	Hour	Summary of Events and Information	Remarks and references to Appendices
	1916 Jany 1st		The Colonel and Orderly Officer visited all Batteries in the Group and Midlothian Battery	
	2nd		Lieut Thomson went to Artillery Course at Invernice	
	3rd		The Doctor left Albert to go on to the Arm as rebilling officer	
	4th		Lectures of 1st & 2nd Batteries relieved by Sections of 4th & 6th Batteries 161 Brigade R.F.A. Ammunition Columns left today for S. Laurent. Brigade Headquarters and Colonel, Adjutant, Clerk and two tebphonists left Albert for Warloy.	
			Remaining Sections of 1st & 2nd left Batteries relieved. Battery Commanders & one Subaltern, 1 N.C.O. per gun and two tebphonists remained.	
	7th		One Section of Midlothian Battery relieved by a Section of Battery of 125 Brigade R.F.A. 2 Sections of Midlothian Battery relieved. Major Anderson, Lieut Buchan, 1 N.C.O. per gun and 2 telephonists remained in the Brigade. Midlothian moving via 1st & 2nd Batteries left Warloy for St Laurent, arriving same afternoon.	
	8th		Midlothian Battery left Albert for S. Laurent arriving same afternoon.	
	9th		The Colonel, Adjutant, Clerk & an Assistant from Brigade Headquarters and two men from 1st & 2nd Batteries left Warloy to join the Brigade at S. Laurent, arriving same afternoon. N.C.O. and men taken in Motor Bus. Colonel & Adjutant rode.	

JANUARY 1916   1/1st Lowland FA Brigade   Army Form C. 2118.

WAR DIARY
or
INTELLIGENCE SUMMARY.
(Erase heading not required.)

Place	Date	Hour	Summary of Events and Information	Remarks and references to Appendices
	1916			
	Jan 10		2/Lieutenant A.F. Maclagan left for England	
	12th		Horse lines cleaning up village and making horse standings	
	14th		2/Lieut Turner returned from Amiens	
	16th		2/Lieut Morren went to Amiens	
	18th		2/Lieut Katzlinem reported from Amiens	
	19th		Battery commanders & other ranks relieved from firing line	
	25th		2/Lieut Morren returned from Amiens	
	30th		2/Lieut Lawen went to Amiens	
	31st		Colonel went home on leave	

J. Kerr Moray Lieut Col.
Commanding 1/1st Lowland F.A. Brigade

FEBRUARY 1916

WAR DIARY
or
INTELLIGENCE SUMMARY.
(Erase heading not required.)

Army Form C. 2118.

/Lt Colonel F.A. Bright/

Place	Date	Hour	Summary of Events and Information	Remarks and references to Appendices
	1916 26 Feb		First party of men two months leave on re-engagement left for home	
			2/Lieut Capel reported from home	
	27		Fresh party (Officer/Major Inches) + 9 R.O.R. men left for 9 days leave	
	28		Fr. Beer went on 9 days leave	
			2/Lieut Patterson returned from Div. Ammn. Col. hired from front	
	29		Major Robertson went to Senior Officers' course at Bernard	
			Brigade moved from St. Laurent to Bruay. The Brow handed over billets to 29th Brigade R.F.A. (G. Division)	
			1 Officer (Major Mackinlay) + 9 men went on 9 days leave	
			Lieut. Dick R.H., Robinson A. Perkins M., Watson F.E., Mitchell L.A., + Lincoln 2/ Lieut in his stamp	
			School attached	
			Lieuts Robertson, Sinclair + Milne left to join 30th Division Artillery	
			Colonel returned from leave	
	1 Mar		Lieut N S Hair + /Lt Jackie reported to be attached; Major Anderson returned from Bernard	
	12		Colonel went to Senior Officers' course at Bernard	
	13		Lewis returned from leave	

WAR DIARY
or
INTELLIGENCE SUMMARY.
(Erase heading not required.)

Army Form C. 2118.

Instructions regarding War Diaries and Intelligence Summaries are contained in F. S. Regs., Part II. and the Staff Manual respectively. Title pages will be prepared in manuscript.

Place	Date	Hour	Summary of Events and Information	Remarks and references to Appendices
	1916 24th July		Adjutant went to Suzanne to see arrangements to to taking over from 149 Brigade R.F.A. (30th Division)	
		11am	Adjutant returned. 1 Officer (Major Anderson) and 8 men went on 9 days leave	
		12th	Colonel returned from Renwick	
			Major Inches went up to Suzanne to start taking over battery positions	
			Captain Mitchell & me Lieutenant Paulin went to Bray to see it 149 Ammunition Column	
		19th	9 Carts moved 9.30 11. 6. 03 men proceeded to Bray to dig alternative gun pits	
			Major Blackaday returned from leave	
		20th	Captain Mackaulay & Nobleman Poke went to Suzanne to take over positions for Middletown & 2nd Batteries	
		21st	Colonel & Orderly Officer & 2 trumpeters went to Suzanne	
			Captain Lane Lieut Jackson & Right Section of 1st Battery went up	
		22nd	2 Officers (2nd Lieut Mitchell Snow & Bright Ford) and 9 men went on 9 days leave	
			9 men from Brigade Headquarters went to Suzanne. One Section of 2nd Middleton Battery went into position	
		24th	At times shelled	

Army Form C. 2118.

WAR DIARY
or
INTELLIGENCE SUMMARY.
(Erase heading not required.)

Instructions regarding War Diaries and Intelligence Summaries are contained in F. S. Regs., Part II. and the Staff Manual respectively. Title pages will be prepared in manuscript.

Place	Date	Hour	Summary of Events and Information	Remarks and references to Appendices
	1916 Feb 26		Remainder of Brigade moved into position at Lizerne	
		10 A.M.	Colonel took over command of Right Group from Lt Colonel Bentley and Battery Commanders took over with their own Batteries. We have the French on our right across the Canal and the 1st Highland F.A. Brigade to the group on our left.	
			The Infantry of the 30th Division were left in front of us.	
		7 P.M.	Enemy started a spasmodic bombardment of Battery positions & Group Headquarters consisting of groups of four or 6 rounds at intervals of 20 minutes to half an hour, lasting till 11 P.M.	
			As the enemy shells fired round Battery positions & Group Headquarters. At 9 P.M. Wiltshires Battery turned on to shell enemy infantry attack on Turko effects which was successfully accomplished	
	28th	1 A.M.	Orders received to move back to Henry lu Dozures tonight.	
			Brigade arrived Henry lu Dozures	
			Brigade moved to Villers Rouge	

J.H. Linton
Kommel ½ at Cowland F.A. Bde.

NO DIARIES
FOR MARCH
& APRIL
1916

WAR DIARY or INTELLIGENCE SUMMARY

Army Form C. 2118.

2608/1 RFA
aee 257
Appx to Vol 8

Place	Date	Hour	Summary of Events and Information	Remarks and references to Appendices
In the field	May 1		The following letter was received from G.O.C, 51st Division. To C.R.A. 51st Division. 51st (G) D. No G/411. The G.O.C. wishes you to convey to the Officers N.C.O's men & the Centre Group his congratulations on the prompt & energetic action during the attack on the morning of 28th inst. Information received from various sources confirms the Impression that the German losses were severe. The G.O.C. considers that it was largely owing to the quickness & intensity of our Artillery fire that the enemy failed to develop a much more serious attack. 29-4-16. Sgd. Dan Stewart. Lt Colonel General Staff. 51st Division. Headquarters Centre Artillery Group. For your information. Sgd. Walsh. Major R.A. Brigade Major. 51st Divisional Arty. 30-4-16.	
	8		Sea Centre Group consisted of 1st Portland Brigade & the 2nd Renfrews 4.5 Hows. Battery of the 3rd Highland (How) Brigade. Front quiet except for some enemy Trench Mortar shooting and consequent retaliation by us to silence the Mortars. MM	
	9		Enemy craters & trenches bombarded by heavy artillery & two guns. D Battery received their gun magazine. MM	
10-14			Front normally quiet. MM	

WAR DIARY or INTELLIGENCE SUMMARY

Army Form C. 2118.

Place	Date	Hour	Summary of Events and Information	Remarks and references to Appendices
The Field	May 15		Re-arrangement of Divisional Artillery. Our D Battery along with D Batteries of 1st & 2nd Highland Brigade becomes a 3. 18 pr battery RHA under Lt Col. Macfarlane. We become 257 Brigade with 2nd Renfrew Battery as D Battery. Our Brigade Ammunition Column becomes No 5 Section DAC. The Division is extending its front Northwards to about 15th Divisional full our 152 Infantry Brigade and our Group are to take over line at Neuville St Vaast. We are to form part of a Left Group with A and U Batteries RHA under Lt Col Chaplain R.H.A. MM	
	16.		New grouping arrangements altered. Left Group now to consist of 4 batteries viz A, B, and C/258 (but see D Battery) and is to be commanded by Lt Col. Macfarlane. MM	
	17.		5th Scaforths had a successful raid supported by our fire. B(2nd Coy) and C(2nd) positions heavily shelled but no damage done. MM	
	19.		One section of A, B, C, D Batteries and C/258 relieved one section of C/110, C/111, A/110, C/113 & B/111 respectively. MM	
	20.		A Battery but single gun into ground position to fire North on trenches on Vimy Ridge. MM	
	21.		About 3.40 p.m. enemy started a heavy bombardment on new area followed by infantry attack on Vimy Ridge in which they were successful. The relief of the remaining sections which was to have been carried out was cancelled about 3.30 p.m. But B/257 and C/258 had reached their relief before the orders reached them. MM	

WAR DIARY
or
INTELLIGENCE SUMMARY
(Erase heading not required.)

Army Form C. 2118.

Place	Date	Hour	Summary of Events and Information	Remarks and references to Appendices
Mhx	21 contd		Position stands B/257 and C/258 under Headquarters 111 Bde, one section A, C & D/257 under Headquarters 110 Bde. The old Anker Group consists of B/258 (old D Battery of 2 Highr under Capt. Shepherd) in B/257 old position left section A/258 (old D Battery of 1st High. under Capt. Edwards, and one sub-section A/257 in A/257 old position.	
	23.		The sections in 2nd Duncan Area had a very busy night and were bombarded with lachrymatory shells. /MM B/258 went under Col. Ryan, left section of C/257 and composite battery of A/258 & A/257 went under Col. Duncan and Headquarters no command of two Battery recalled from 25th Div area and divided into two Groups. Right Group under Col. Macfarlane consisting of 256 & 258 Brigades Left Group under Col. Duncan consisting of 255 & 257 Brigades A.R. Batteries go to their old positions. D. Battery go to divisional position occupied at one time by D/112. C go into old French position to right and change with C/255 to-morrow. /MM	
	27.		Lieut. Col. Findlay went home on Medical certificate.	
	28.		Lieut. Col. Seligman from 4th Division to command the Brigade /MM Early this morning enemy exploded a mine & attempted a small attack. The front was quiet again by about 2.45 am. /MM	

WAR DIARY
or
INTELLIGENCE SUMMARY

(Erase heading not required.)

Army Form C. 2118.

Place	Date	Hour	Summary of Events and Information	Remarks and references to Appendices
	May 30		"A" battery position heavily shelled. By 5 9" + 8" one gun completely destroyed. Brigade started to move back into position to relieve 258th Brigade. A B + C/257 + C/258 relieved C/110, C/111, A/110 + B/111 respectively, with one section.	
	31		Remaining sections moved into new positions 2/257 remaining in old position for special scheme. Brigade Headquarters moved to Berthonval Farm to "take over" from 110 Bde. Lt. Col. (Buckley D.S.O. and 113 (How) Bde. Lt. Col. Pegg Group consists of A B + C/257, C/258, D/111, 1 2/112 both Hows.)	

257th (Northumbrian) Brigade R.F.A.

WAR DIARY or INTELLIGENCE SUMMARY

Army Form C. 2118.

Place	Date	Hour	Summary of Events and Information	Remarks and references to Appendices
In the Field.	June 2.		Enemy put up heavy barrage on Infantry trenches. We put on a counter barrage from 8.1 a.m. to 9.15 a.m. when the front was knocked quiet. B/110 and B/113 took 18/pr Batteries of 25th Division and sent back to be rendered fit for group.	
	3-15.		Very little Artillery work done as Infantry wanted to strengthen their trenches and make some good dug-outs for the men. During this period Brigade numbers changed from 257 to 260. A/119 (38th Division) relieved B/113.	
	16.		One section C/120, D/120 & D/122 (38th Division) relieved one section B/110, D/111 & D/112 (25th Division).	
	17.		Remaining sections of above batteries exchanged.	
	18-23		Front normally quiet.	
	24.		A few positions shelled — Gun pits knocked about — very little damage done.	
	26.		German raiding party repulsed. Artillery fire reported very effective.	
	27.		One section of A/303, B/303, D/303, D/305 (60th Div Arty) relieved one section of C/120, A/119, D/122, D/112 respectively.	
	28.		Running actions of above batteries exchanged.	
	30.		Colonel Adjutant 300 Bde (60th Div Arty) attached.	
			During this month very little artillery fire took place or Infantry requests.	

Arthur M. Matthews Capt for Lt Col Cmdg
260th (Lowland) Brigade R.F.A.

Confidential
No 3097/A
HIGHLAND DIVISION

Vol 10

Confidential
War Diary
of
260th Brigade R.F.A.
Shown on 258 Mays June
From 1st July 1916 to 31st July 1916

(Volume)

War Diary
260th (Lowland) Brigade R.F.A.

1916

July 2. About 12·45 A.M. the Batteries opened fire on their barrage in answer to Heavy bombardment of our trenches. About 2.15 A.M Infantry reported enemy attack when rate of fire was increased. A steady barrage was maintained till 2·45 A.M when Infantry reported that attack had failed and front was quiet. Considerable damage is reported to have been done to the enemy trenches by our Artillery fire.

13. Up to date this month the Howitzers in the Group have been successful in knocking out snipers' Posts, and other enemy work in craters. The G.O.C. has congratulated the Group Commander on good work done. Except for retaliation for Trench Mortar fire little else has taken place. Batteries have been working to strengthen gun positions.

14. Group Headquarters handed over to Lieut. Colonel Baillie D.S.O. 303rd Brigade, R.F.A. 60th Divisional Artillery. 51st Divisional Artillery pulled out of line.

15. At 6·40 A.M. Brigade left Wagon Line at HAUTE AVESNES and marched to MILLY arriving there about 12·30 P.M.

16. 9 A.M. Left MILLY for LE MEILLARD arriving there about 1 p.m.

19. 9 A.M. Left LE MEILLARD arriving VIGNACOURT about 1·30 A.M.

20. 5·45 P.M. Left VIGNACOURT arriving DERNANCOURT at 4·15 A.M. via FLESSELLS, RAINECOURT, QUERRIEUX, HEILLY and RIBEMONT.

21.

Page. 2.

War Diary. (Continued)

1916

July 21. CRA and Brigade Commanders went up line.

22. Colonel, Orderly Officer, 2 officers per battery went up to see new positions.

2nd Lieut. Steedman missing.

23. Brigade took over from 80th Brigade. The 5th Division are on our Right and 19th on our Left. 51st Divisional Artillery are at present "Corps Artillery" and not directly covering any particular Infantry.

24. Brigade Headquarters and Batteries all heavily shelled. Brigade moved to take over positions of 96th Brigade RFA just near Mametz Wood and behind Bazentin le Grand.

2/Lieut. Steedman now reported wounded in Hospital. 51st Divisional Artillery ceased to be Corps Artillery and are now covering our own Infantry. Our brigade is responsible for part of the line just east of High Wood.

25. 2/Lieut. Lamond wounded.

26. Major Anderson and 2/Lieut. Mitchell wounded.

27. Supported 5th Division in attack on DELVILLE WOOD.

29. Joined in bombardment of enemy lines from 3 P.M. to 3.30 P.M. We took on trench east of HIGH WOOD and searched back.

30. 153rd Infantry Brigade attacked enemy lines east of High Wood. Not successful owing to heavy machine gun fire. Yesterday's bombardment was repeated this morning from 3.45 A.M. to 5.15 A.M. Since coming into action Batteries have fired every night searching from Barrage Zone and back to and including distant enemy approaches to SWITCH TRENCH east of High Wood.

Major Anderson returned to duty —

51st Divisional Artillery.

260th BRIGADE

ROYAL FIELD ARTILLERY

AUGUST 1 9 1 6

WAR DIARY or INTELLIGENCE SUMMARY

Army Form C. 2118.

BRITISH WAR
No 21 (A)
HIGHLAND DIVISION

Place	Date 1916 August	Hour	Summary of Events and Information	Remarks and references to Appendices
In Field	1.		18th Battalion moved forward to position for cutting wire in front of Switch Trench East of High Wood. "C" Battery was split up making "A" and "B" Batteries into 6 Gun Batteries. Major Anderson went to Krags's West Brigade. Lieut Cave changed a little further South in Wood Lane Trench. Night firing 1000 rounds 18pdr and 166 rounds 4.5" Howitzers for Brigade. On German front line and Much Area.	
	2		Brigade Headquarters moved forward to position near 18th Batteries. Bombardment Scheme carried out on strong point at East corner of HIGH WOOD And area just East of it. One Howitzer Battery only took part firing about 130 rounds from 4.15 p.m. to 5.20 a.m. At 5:30 p.m. to 7 p.m. a second scheme in which Wood Lane Trench was bombarded from High Wood to a point about 800 yards N.W. of Longueval was carried out by the Divisional Artillery at a rate of fire of 1 round per gun per two minutes. Night firing 500 rounds 18pdr. and 166 rounds 4.5" Howitzers for Brigade.	
	3.		Bombardment of West side of High Wood carried out from 9.5 a.m. to 11.10 A.M by Divisional Artillery And Heavy Howitzers. Our 18pdr Batteries again all went off this scheme owing to their expressed position for wire cutting purposes. Night firing same as last night.	
	4.		Infantry attack on enemy lines South End of Wood Lane Trench. 51st Artillery Assisted in bombardment starting at 12 midnight 2/3rd until mid 8/25 6 4.5" Hows, taken up at 2 p.m. yesterday by 29/260 who continued till hour of attack – 12.40 A.M. This morning 20 rounds per battery per hour from 12.40 A.M. till 2.40 A.M. this rate was increased by both above batteries firing at the rate of 60 rounds per hour from 10.25AM to 9.	

WAR DIARY
or
INTELLIGENCE SUMMARY

(Erase heading not required.)

Instructions regarding War Diaries and Intelligence Summaries are contained in F. S. Regs., Part II. and the Staff Manual respectively. Title Pages will be prepared in manuscript.

Place	Date 1916 August	Hour	Summary of Events and Information	Remarks and references to Appendices
	4 (contind.)	to 11.35 AM	A bombardment was carried out on north corner of High Wood and ground just east back to Switch trench, in which our Howitzer Battery took part. Another bombardment, none of Kontain Batteries took part.	
		4.45pm to 5.50 pm	From 9 PM tonight Brigade HQ moved further down Wood Lane trench. Enemy when allotted for destroying enemy work and searching communications by day 4.15 rounds do 18hr. and 2.33 h.S. trench; by night 500 rounds do 18hr. and 166 h.S. Howitzers. Per Brigade. This to be fired in addition to observed fire, killing attacks of special bombardments. Bombardment of 2nd inst repeated AM from	
	5.	11AM to 11·50AM	"bombardment	
		4.20 PM to 5.10 PM	Yesterday afternoon's repeated. This only affected one Howitzer Battery. Ordinary day and night firing according to Yesterday's orders.	
	6.	9.5AM to 10 AM	The 255th and 256th Brigade carried out a bombardment of High Wood and ground to N.E. and from	
		2.20pm to 2.29pm	they bombarded North End of Wood Lane trench and parts of Switch trench.	
			Division for Artillery released by 33rd Division. Divisional Artillery	
	7/8		now under orders of G.O.C. 33rd Division. Day and night firing as usual.	

WAR DIARY
or
INTELLIGENCE SUMMARY
(Erase heading not required.)

Place	Date 1916 August	Hour	Summary of Events and Information	Remarks and references to Appendices
	7.	5.30 pm 6.30 pm	Our Brig 9th pickard in bombardment of Enemy trench (orchard Trench) running NE from South End of Wood Lane. Ammunition 18 hrs 9c rounds per gun. H.S. How 60 rounds per gun. Ammunition which for night firing tonight to assist XIII Corps operations. JC	
	8.		2/Lieut Fortune M reported for duty. Orders for special registration of zone NW of Delville Wood. Day and night firing as usual. JC	
	9.		The section of each battery relieved by one section of each battery 48th Brigade. 14th Divisional Artillery guns were pulled out. Relief carried out without any incident. JC	
	10.		Registration of new sectors Next morning action relieved command handed over to Lieut Colonel Boxall. Brigade remained at Argon Luise.	
	11.		Since coming into action in the South the Batteries have been constantly under fire and also the drivers coming up with ammunition. JC	

WAR DIARY or INTELLIGENCE SUMMARY

(Erase heading not required.)

Instructions regarding War Diaries and Intelligence Summaries are contained in F.S. Regs., Part II. and the Staff Manual respectively. Title Pages will be prepared in manuscript.

Place	Date 1916 August	Hour	Summary of Events and Information	Remarks and references to Appendices
The Valle	11		Divisional Artillery moved to Bonnay. Largo guns behind FRICOURT at 9 A.M. arriving BONNAY 1 p.m. JS	
	14		Brigade entrained at SALEUX just south of Amiens on 13th – 14th March from BONNAY to SALEUX carried out by Batteries. Detrained at ARQUES just south east of ST. OMER and marched to LYNDE. JS	
	16		One section of each Battery took over line from FRELINGHIEM Sect. from 3rd Brigade N.Z.F.A. JS	
	17		2nd Section relief complete. Command taken over from Lieut. Colonel Standish. JS	
	18		Front very quiet. Batteries registering. JS	
	19		Registration continued. A little hostile Shellfire and T.M. fire occurred during the evening. JS	
	20		Registration continued. Observed front very quiet. Colonel Seligman left to take up appointment as C.R.A. 7th Divisional Artillery. Major Onslow took over temporary command. JS	
	21		Registration continued. Front quiet. JS	
	22		Some slight enemy movement observed. Front quiet. Registration continued. AJ	

INTELLIGENCE SUMMARY

(Erase heading not required.)

Instructions regarding War Diaries and Intelligence Summaries are contained in F.S. Regs., Part II. and the Staff Manual respectively. Title Pages will be prepared in manuscript.

Place	Date 1916	Hour	Summary of Events and Information	Remarks and references to Appendices
	22 (continued)		"A" Battery tried to register a front by aeroplane observation but light was too bad. JR	
	23		Divisional Artillery reorganised. Midlothian Battery split up on one section going to 1st City of Edinburgh making it a one gun battery (A/260) and one section to 2nd City of Edinburgh making it also a six gun battery (B/260). Major Anderson takes command of No. 1 Section RA.C. 256th Brigade. Major Reid takes command of No. 1 Section RA.C. 256th Brigade. Lt.Col. F.T. Oldham takes over command of the Brigade and Lt.Col. Scroggie commanding 153 Infantry Brigade JR. C Batteries 256 Brigade covering 153 Infantry Brigade JR.	
	24		260th Brigade Batteries carried out successful registration by aeroplane observation. Ordinary registration continued. JR	
	25 26 3/31		Front very quiet during period. Batteries engaged in registering and instructing Young Officers and NCO's in the Country behind the enemy lines. Occasional movement has been fired on	

2449 Wt. W14957/M90 750,000 1/16 J.B.C. & A. Forms/C.2118/12.

E. E. Ostiaur
Com.dt Dep.t (Lanark.) Brigade
R.F.A.

Army Form C. 2118.

WAR DIARY
or
INTELLIGENCE SUMMARY

(Erase heading not required.)

Instructions regarding War Diaries and Intelligence Summaries are contained in F. S. Regs, Part II. and the Staff Manual respectively. Title Pages will be prepared in manuscript.

Place	Date 1916 September	Hour	Summary of Events and Information	Remarks and references to Appendices
The Field.	1		In the morning about 1 A.m. enemy put up heavy barrage along the front to which we replied. Front reported quiet by 2 a.m.	JS.
	3		Battery out wire satisfactorily in three places. Most reported very deep. 2/Lieut. L. Shayock proceeded to 2nd Army Signalling School. 2/Lieut. S.A. Salmon assumed duties of orderly officer temporarily.	JS.
	4		"B" Battery cut wire in one place during afternoon. Batteries engaged	JS.
	5-8		Front very quiet during the period in instructing young officers and N.C.O's. Occasional movement fired on.	JS.
	9		Headquarters Horse Lines moved to PONT NIEPPE. "A" Battery Horse Lines Removed from ARMENTIERES to PONT NIEPPE	JS.

WAR DIARY
or
INTELLIGENCE SUMMARY

(Erase heading not required.)

Army Form C. 2118.

Place	Date	Hour	Summary of Events and Information	Remarks and references to Appendices
	10.		Brigade Headquarters moved out to rest for 10 days. Up to date very little firing has been done and the front has been very quiet except on the one or two reconnre details.	JL
	13.		D Battery Wagon Lines moved to near EPINETTE.	
	15.		Headquarters Horse lines moved from PONT NIEPPE to near STEENWERCK. Batteries took part in bombardment - covering Infantry Raids in the evening.	JL JL
	16-19		Front very quiet.	
	20.		Brigade Headquarters returned to ARMENTIERES to take over Left Group from 256 Brigade Headquarters. Captain Scott took over command of D/280 Battery. Lieut Ollis 25-6 Brigade remained as adjutant Left Group until 2/Lieut Stimock's return from 2nd Army Signalling Course.	JL

WAR DIARY or INTELLIGENCE SUMMARY

Army Form C. 2118.

Place	Date	Hour	Summary of Events and Information	Remarks and references to Appendices
	22.		Australian Field Artillery Brigade arrived to take over Left Group. "A" Battery relieved by 1section 50th Australian Battery. "C" section " " " 51st " " "B" " " " " "	
	23.		"C" Section proceeded to VIEUX BERQUIN. "A" section "A" Battery relieved by 1 section 50th Brigade. 1st section "B" Battery relieved by 1 section 51st Brigade. These sections and remaining sections of 78th Batteries along with "B" Battery proceeded — to join other sections at LA COURONNE between VIEUX and NEUF BERQUIN	
	24.		2/Lieut. Thomas Sturrock returned from 2nd Army Signalling School and assumed duties of adjutant.	

WAR DIARY
or
INTELLIGENCE SUMMARY
(Erase heading not required.)

Army Form C. 2118.

Place	Date	Hour	Summary of Events and Information	Remarks and references to Appendices
	25.		Brigade left 9 A.M. and marched to HURIONVILLE via ROBECQ, LILLERS, BURBERE arriving at 3 p.m.	J.S.
	26.		Brigade left HURIONVILLE 9 A.M. and marched to EPS via PERNES arriving 1.30 p.m.	J.S.
	27.		Brigade left EPS 8 A.M. and marched to BOUBERS-SUR-CANCHE via CROISETTE arriving 2 p.m. 2/Lt Entwistry went to Hospital.	J.S.
	28.	7 A.M.	Brigade left BOUBERS-SUR-CANCHE and marched to BUS-LES-ARTOIS via BOUVIERES, BARLY, OCCOCHES, DOULLENS and SARTON arriving 4 p.m.	J.S.
	29.	9 A.M.	Brigade left BUS-LES-ARTOIS and marched to PUCHVILLERS via LOUVENCOURT ARQUEVES and RAINCHEVAL arriving 12 noon.	J.S.

Place	Date	Hour	Summary of Events and Information	Remarks and references to Appendices
	30		2/Lieut. S A Salveson proceeded on leave. One section of each 18 Pr. Battery and one section Howitzer Battery relieved corresponding sections of Batteries of 49th Divisional Artillery in positions N.E. of MESNIL.	

J Maurice Throck
Lieut. Colonel
Commdg. 2nd/1st (Rowland) Brigade R.F.A

L381

Headquarters.
51st Divl Arty.

I regret that I have no copies of form for War Diary - these are on indent but have not yet come to hand.

3-8-16.

Herbert West
Captain
for Lieut Colonel
Comdg 260 Brigade R.F.A

CONFIDENTIAL.
No 21/1
HIGHLAND
DIVISION.

Vol 12

WAR DIARY
of
261st (Lowland) BRIGADE, R.F.A.
for
SEPTEMBER 1916.

CONFIDENTIAL.
No 21/A
HIGHLAND DIVISION.

51 Div

Vol 13

WAR DIARY
of
260th (Lowland) Brigade R.F.A.

From 1st to 31st October 1916.

1
Confidential.

WAR DIARY or INTELLIGENCE SUMMARY

Army Form C. 2118.

Place	Date 1916 (October)	Hour	Summary of Events and Information	Remarks and references to Appendices
The Field.	1.		Brigade Headquarters and Batteries moved to HEDAUVILLE. 1 Section "A" Battery, 1 Section "B" Battery and 1 Section "D" Battery relieved corresponding sections of A/246, B/246 and D/246 Batteries 49th Divisional Artillery.	
	2.		Lieut Colonel F.J. Oldham took over command of Left Group from Lieut Colonel Clifford (West Riding) 49th Divisional Artillery. Group consists of A, B, D Batteries of 260th Brigade and B/85th Battery of 18th Divisional Artillery. Night barrage of 100 rounds per hour per Brigade fired on Strasburg Trench and communication Trench connecting.	
	3.		Day wet and misty. Observation very difficult. Registration carried out on German trenches as far as conditions would permit. Barrage for 10 minutes of 1 round per gun per minute carried out during infantry attack on night of B/85th Battery removed from Left Group at 6 p.m. to 18th Division. Night fired continuous slow barrage on enemy trench communications carried out through out night.	
	4.		Day wet and misty. Slow barrage of 2 salvoes per hour per Battery carried out during infantry attack on night, night firing as before.	
	5.		"D"/260 Battery took part in Barrage of Serre Road during Infantry Attack on Schwaben Redoubt. Registration carried out.	
		P.M 1/1.45	Lieut Oldham accompanied General Oldham to visit proposed new positions near HEBUTERNE. Orders received from Divisional Artillery to vacate all Battery positions after 2AM next morning.	

WAR DIARY or INTELLIGENCE SUMMARY

Army Form C. 2118.

Place	Date	Hour	Summary of Events and Information	Remarks and references to Appendices
In Field	6	10 p.m.	Guns and howitzers pulled out and all positions vacated. Guns and detachments marched to wagon lines at HEDAUVILLE. Motor lorries captured enemy guns from forward positions near HEBUTERNE.	J.C.
		2 pm	Brigade left HEDAUVILLE and marched to BUS-LES-ARTOIS via FORCEVILLE and BERTRAM COURT arriving 4.30 p.m.	J.C.
	7		Motor lorries captured Battery positions.	J.C.
	9		Night work commenced on Battery position. Again reconnoitred new positions. Battery ready to move into new positions.	J.C.
	10		Work on Battery position continued.	J.C.
	11		"D" Battery took up position in valley between COLIN CAMPS and HEBUTERNE. and was under Lieut Colonel CRAVEN 169th Brigade R.F.A. for tactics. Work continued on 18 pdr positions.	J.C.
	12.		2/Lt G.A. Salman returned from leave.	J.C.
	12-14		Batteries engaged in preparing positions &c.	J.C.
	15		Order received to stop all work on positions.	J.C.
	16	9.15 a.m.	A/260 Battery withdrawn from line.	
		18 pdr	Batteries engaged during night with help of D.A.C. in removing ammunition from forward positions.	J.C.

WAR DIARY
or
INTELLIGENCE SUMMARY
(Erase heading not required.)

Army Form C. 2118.

Place	Date	Hour	Summary of Events and Information	Remarks and references to Appendices
"In Field"	1916 (Notes) 17		Lieut. W. H. Harvey rejoined from Base Hospital. Lieut. Colonel Oldham and Adjutant proceeded to MAILLY-MAILLET to reconnoitre for positions in front of BEAUMONT-HAMEL. "A" (4 guns) "B" and "D" Batteries proceeded later to MAILLY-MAILLET to take up positions there.	
	18	5 AM	"A" Battery took over position (4 guns) at Q.14.a.9.6 from A/179 Bde R.F.A. "B" and "D" Batteries took up vacant positions in front of Mailly-Maillet	
		5 PM	Registration completed.	
	19.	6 (AM)	Wagon lines moved from BUS-LES-ARTOIS to VARENNES. Orders received for wire cutting on support and third line trenches behind Zone. Battery commanders engaged in selecting suitable O.P's. "A" Battery only were in the afternoon.	
	20.		Night firing on approaches to Zone carried out by "A" and "B" Batteries. Allotment 200 rounds for battery formation.	

WAR DIARY or INTELLIGENCE SUMMARY

Army Form C. 2118.

Place	Date	Hour	Summary of Events and Information	Remarks and references to Appendices
The Field	1916 20th Oct		Formation of No 3 Group consisting of 168th Bde (32nd Divisional Artillery) and 260th Bde. Group under command of Lieut Colonel Witham with Zone slightly altered to farther north. Lieut Colonel Fitz Maurice (168th Brigade) and Battery Commanders moved to recon noitre for positions. Wire cutting carried out by "A" "B" "C" Batteries 260th Brigade during morning and afternoon.	
	21		Wire cutting by batteries on my front and 3rd Line trenches. Night firing on approaches to zone by 18pdr Batteries. Allotment 150 rounds H.E. each. Registration carried out by 168th Brigade Batteries.	
	22		Wire cutting continued by all batteries of 260th Brigade. Registration continued by 168th Brigade. Two bursts of fire each for 3 minutes carried out by all No 3 Group Batteries at 11.5 p.m. and 12.35 A.M. (23rd inst) to cover wire cutting by infantry in front line with Bangalore torpedoes.	
	23	6-6.15 p.m.	Batteries bombarded enemy's trenches with H.E. rate 1 round per gun per minute. Wire cutting carried out by all batteries of group. Long ranges night map shooting.	

WAR DIARY
or
INTELLIGENCE SUMMARY

(Erase heading not required.)

Army Form C. 2118.

Place	Date	Hour	Summary of Events and Information	Remarks and references to Appendices
The Field	19/6 24		More Cutting programme proceeded with. Day hot and misty — all ough shooting.	
			Night firing by A & B Batteries 260th Brigade on approaches to zone allotment 150 rds per battery. Bursts of fire by 2 batteries 168th Brigade during evening to cover noise of approach of tanks.	
			2/Lt Bruce proceeded on leave.	
	25.	A.M. 6:15	Short bursts of fire for 3 minutes each carried out by Group at 11.5 p.m. and 12.35 A.M. (25th inst.) to cover men getting by barbed wire defences.	K.
			Burst of fire at 1 round per gun per minute by all batteries of Group on enemy's trenches.	
			Registration of reviewed front carried out by Batteries.	K.
		7 p.m.	Raid by 7th Argyll and Sutherland Highlanders on crater Q.10.b.7.8. Barrage supplied by A and B Batteries 260 Brigade and B/168 Battery. Fire started at 2 rounds per gun for 15 minutes — after 15 minutes 1 round per gun per minute continued till 8.6 p.m. when signal to cease fire given.	K.
		9.30 p.m	Raid renewed. Fire supplied by "A" and "B" Batteries 260 th Brigade at rate of 2 rounds per gun per minute. Continued till 10.20 p.m. when order to cease fire given. Raiding party returned without identification. Bursts of fire again carried out by 2 batteries 168th Brigade to cover approach of tanks.	

Army Form C. 2118.

WAR DIARY
or
INTELLIGENCE SUMMARY
(Erase heading not required.)

Instructions regarding War Diaries and Intelligence Summaries are contained in F. S. Regs., Part II. and the Staff Manual respectively. Title Pages will be prepared in manuscript.

Place	Date 1916 October	Hour	Summary of Events and Information	Remarks and references to Appendices
The Field	26	A.M. 6-6.15	Burst of fire by all Group Batteries following trenches. Rate 1 round per gun per minute.	JB
			Wire cutting continued	JB
		P.M. 5.30	Stoke Battery took part in bombardment in connection with Infantry raid. Ordinary night firing carried out — 300 rounds expended.	JB
	27	A.M. 6-6.15	Burst of fire carried out. Wire cutting continued.	JB
			Ordinary night firing — 300 rounds.	JB
	28	A.M. 6-6.15	Burst of fire carried out. Wire cutting considerably hampered by strong wind.	JB
		P.M. 11.25	B/240 C/168 and D/168 Batteries took part in bombardment ordered by R.E. Rate of fire 2 rounds per gun per minute. Each battery had opened fire on approaches to Koue.	JB
			Night firing as usual. 2nd Lieut Allan G Simson reported from Base Hospital.	JB
	29	A.M. 6-6.15	Burst of fire. Wire cutting continued. Night firing as usual.	JB

Army Form C. 2118.

WAR DIARY
or
INTELLIGENCE SUMMARY
(Erase heading not required.)

Place	Date	Hour	Summary of Events and Information	Remarks and references to Appendices
The Field	10/16 Octor. 30		Night firing as usual. Wire cutting continued.	
	31	6.45 6.50	Burst of fire by all Group Batteries. Night firing as usual. Wire cutting continued.	

Norman [signature]
2/Lt.
for Lieut. Colonel
Comdg. 160th (New Zealand) Bde R.F.A.
1-11-16.

Confidential

Vol 14

WAR DIARY

of

260th (Lowland) BRIGADE, R.F.A.

From 1 November 1916
to 30 November 1916

WAR DIARY or INTELLIGENCE SUMMARY

Army Form C. 2118.

Place	Date 1916 November	Hour	Summary of Events and Information	Remarks and references to Appendices
The HOH	1	6.10/6.15 P.M.	Special bombardment of wire by Group Batteries at rate of 3 rounds per gun per minute.	J.F.
			Wire cutting continued during the day. Night firing as usual.	J.F.
	2		Wire cutting as usual. Night firing as usual.	J.F.
	3	6.40&6.45 A.M.	Special bombardment of wire and trenches.	J.F.
			Wire cutting continued. Night firing as usual.	
	4	4.30&4.35 P.M.	Special bombardment by whole Group.	J.F.
			Wire cutting by batteries and French mortars. Night firing as usual.	
	5	8.30&8.55 A.M.	Special bombardment.	J.F.
			Night firing as before.	
	6	6.10&6.15 P.M.	Special bombardment.	J.F.
			Night firing as before.	J.F.
	7		2/Lieut. S.H.Webb arrived for duty with the Brigade. Attached to "A" Battery.	J.F.
		5.25 P.M.	Wire cutting continued as before. Raid by 15th Infantry Brigade at R.H.D. 87.02. All batteries in Group engaged and firing was correct on till 6.23 p.m. when assigned to cease fire green.	J.F.
			Night firing as before.	
	8		Wire cutting continued on points reported on by Infantry Patrols.	J.F.
	9		2/Lieut. J.F. Bones reported from leave.	J.F.
	10	5.45&6 A.M.	Special bombardment. Brigade Headquarters shelled with 5.9" in the afternoon. Shelling started at night 11 p.m. with H.E. and Gas (Phosgene).	J.F.
	11	5.45&6 A.M.	Morning bombardment. Wire cutting continued during day but starvation difficult owing to mist.	J.F.
	12	do.	Morning bombardment by whole Group. Enemy's trenches	
			D Battery heavily shelled half an hour later with gas (Phosgene and lachrymatory) and HE shells. Casualties in other ranks 2 killed 1 wounded and gassed and H gassed.	J.F.
			Wire cutting continued all day.	

WAR DIARY or INTELLIGENCE SUMMARY

Army Form C. 2118.

Place	Date	Hour	Summary of Events and Information	Remarks and references to Appendices
In Field	1916 Nov 13		*Attack Beaumont Hamel*	
			Z day. Attack by 51st Division with 2nd Division on left and 63rd Division on right. Attack started at 5.45 A.M. with Artillery Barrage on front line lifting at intervals back to green line through Beaumont Hamel and later to Frankfurt Trench and 150 yards beyond. This lasted till 8.34. Fire on 150 yards beyond Yellow line continued at slow rate for 3 hours when orders to cease fire given (10 minutes fire with 5 minute pauses).	
		1 pm	2 Tanks reported to have entered Beaumont Hamel.	
		2.5 pm	Fire reopened on yellow line and continued at slow rate (1 round per gun per minute).	
		5.45 pm	Rate of fire reduced to ½ round per gun per minute.	
		6.15 pm	Infantry reported to be in possession of green line and consolidating there. Barrage started on line I and J. 1 round per gun every five minutes	
		9 pm	Barrage lifted to line K.	
		9.55 pm	" " " " M. Slow rate of fire kept on this line all night (1 round per gun every five minutes.	
			850 prisoners reported taken by Left Brigade (152). Infantry all ahead highly of Artillery Barrage.	
	14	5.45 A.M.	Attack continued towards Yellow line. Barrage with lifts finishing at 6.20 (2 rounds per gun per minute) on Yellow line at 8.35 A.M. continuously at ½ round per gun per minute and later at ¼ round per gun per minute (A & B/160 Batteries only).	
		1.25 pm	Munich Trench reported to be in our hands.	
		3.45 pm	Barrage reopened on 150 yards beyond Yellow line at 3 rounds per gun per minute gradually decreasing and leaving 256 B and 260 B. Brigades alone barraging Divisional Zone for 3½ hours at slow rate = 18 phr. only. Horn on Beaumont Serre Road	
		5.30 pm 6 pm	260 B Bde relieved of barrage by A/168 Battery. Position still obscure through objective (yellow line) reported to be gained.	
		7.30 pm	Night barrage by whole Group put on 150 yards beyond Yellow line and approaches thereto. Allotment 400 per 18 pdr 450 per How. Battery	

Army Form C. 2118.

WAR DIARY
or
INTELLIGENCE SUMMARY
(Erase heading not required.)

Instructions regarding War Diaries and Intelligence Summaries are contained in F. S. Regs., Part II. and the Staff Manual respectively. Title Pages will be prepared in manuscript.

Place	Date 1916 November	Hour	Summary of Events and Information	Remarks and references to Appendices
The Field	15	12.30 AM	Night firing quickened to 1 round per gun per minute for 10 minutes on report by O. that green rocket had been seen.	
		9 A.M.	Fire opened on barrage behind Munich Trench to cover Infantry attack on Munich Trench and Yellow line lifting till 9.20 to 150 yards behind Yellow line (rate 4 rounds per gun per minute) then decreasing to ½ round per gun. 9.30 A.M. Barrage moved 100 yards.	
		2 p.m.	Rate reduced to ¼ round per gun. 2/Lt Fairley made reconnaissance in Beaumont Hamel and environs — established communication to dug out there — also reconnoitred Station Road for barrage of guns.	
		6.35 p.m.	Night firing 50 yards behind Frankfort Trench — Burst of fire — same time for S.O.S.	
	16	9 A.M.	Slow bursts of fire on S.O.S. barrage during day. 2/Lt Fairley and Allchurch went forward to Beaumont Hamel to establish communication with Coy in front line — report received 10.30 A.M. Lieut Colonel Oldham went to 154 Infantry Brigade Headquarters in white City to relieve Colonel Dixon of liaison duties. Colonel Fitz- maurice took over command of No 3 Group. 2/Lt Thomson proceeded to relieve 2/Lt Fairley and continues laying of wire to front line.	
		4 p.m.	Barrage of 1 round per minute opened on account of numerous German lights being sent up. Rate quickened to 1 round per gun later and at 5 p.m. fire stopped. Night firing as last night.	

WAR DIARY or INTELLIGENCE SUMMARY

Army Form C. 2118.

Place	Date	Hour	Summary of Events and Information	Remarks and references to Appendices
The Field	1916 17 November	3, 4, 5, 7 p.m.	Bursts of fire throughout morning on S.O.S. lines beyond Frankfurt Trench. Bombardments of Munich Trench and Frankfurt Trench by 256 and 260th Bties (18 pdrs, 3 rounds per gun per minute and Howitzers 2 rounds per gun per minute.)	
			168th Brigade withdrawn from the 3 Scouts to join 2nd Division to take up positions in front of Aveluy village.	
		5 p.m.	Lieut Colonel Hilleen returned to Brigade from Liaison duty the 154 Infantry Brigade having been withdrawn from front line. Night firing as before. Lieut W.J. Robertson reported from Base to join unit. Posted to D Battery.	
	18.	6.10 A.M.	Attack by 32nd Division on Munich and Frankfurt Trenches. 51st Divisional Artillery and 2nd and 3rd Divisional Artilleries being engaged. 260 Brigade zone on Munich Trench with 6 18pdr guns opened with 4 rounds per gun per minute then 1 round and later ½ round. (Howrs ½ above rate). After one hour barrage lifted to further north R1A.	
		10.30 A.M.	Barrage brought back to 150 yards beyond Frankfurt Trench. Rate 120 rounds per battery per hour.	
		1 p.m.	Barrage advanced to Munich (6 guns) and Frankfurt Trenches (3 guns) Howitzars being in communications behind. Rate 160 rounds for 18 pdr Battery and 80 rounds for Howitzer battery.	
		1.25 p.m.	Rate reduced by ½.	
		5.30 p.m.	Rate reduced by ½.	
		6 p.m.	Rate reduced to 30 rounds for 18 pdrs. and 15 per Howitzar.	
		6.30 p.m.	Rate reduced to 12 rounds per 18 pdr. and 8 rounds per Howitzar. Night firing on Munich Trench (6 guns) & Frankfurt Trench (3 guns) Howr. on Frankfurt Trench (2 Howrs.) Expd. ammunition (2 Hozrs Col R) Captain Benson 535 Regt Hozrs C (2 Guns) reported at Headquarters.	18

WAR DIARY
or
INTELLIGENCE SUMMARY

Army Form C. 2118.

Place	Date 1916 September	Hour	Summary of Events and Information	Remarks and references to Appendices
The Field	19.		Burst of fire continued on Munich Trench and Frankfurt Trench throughout day. 18 pdrs 12 rounds and Howr 8 rounds per hour. Night firing as above.	
	20.		Bursts of fire continued as above. Major Active proceeded on 10 days leave.	
	21.		Burst of fire continued throughout day.	
		4:30pm	Fire opened on S.O.S. barrage on report of Heavy German shelling on north and south of Hess. Fire quickened to 3 rounds per gun per minute for 5 minutes and then decreased slowly until 5:15 when fire ceased.	
			Night firing stopped. Brigade only responsible for S.O.S. barrage.	
			C/260 engaged in improving gun positions. Lt. Col. Milburn proceeded on 10 days leave.	
	22.		Was received to proceed to take up positions near Courcellette. Gn 24th and 25th.	
	23.		Batteries engaged checking registration of Old Munich Trench. Brigade Commander and orderlies proceeded to Courcellette to view new positions.	
			Brigade pulled out and moved to wagon lines at VARENNES.	
	24.		Brigade moved to new wagon lines north of Albert.	
			1 section personnel of each battery took over from Canadian Artillery near Courcellette.	
	25.		Brigade (Major Acke commanding) took over from 3rd Canadian Brigade 1st Division (Lt Col Leonard). Remaining sections of batteries relieved Canadian Artillery.	
			A Battery relieved 10th Battery (two guns) and 49th Battery (two guns)	
			B " " 11th " (3 guns) " 12th " (three guns)	
			C " " 23rd " (4 Horrs)	
			D " " 22nd " (4 Howr)	

Army Form C. 2118.

WAR DIARY
or
INTELLIGENCE SUMMARY
(Erase heading not required.)

Instructions regarding War Diaries and Intelligence Summaries are contained in F. S. Regs., Part II. and the Staff Manual respectively. Title Pages will be prepared in manuscript.

Place	Date	Hour	Summary of Events and Information	Remarks and references to Appendices
The Field	1916. November 26.		Major Porter attended Conference of Brigade Commanders at Divisional Artillery.	
	27.		Batteries engaged in registration. Night firing 18 pdrs (300 rounds) on trench junctions and communication trenches.	J.F.
	28.		Registration continued. Night firing on Targets 6 and 9A (100 rounds per 18 pdr Battery).	J.F.
			Owing to misty Registration impossible. Night firing as before.	J.F.
			Captain Scott proceeded to England to Gunnery Course at Westcliffe on Sea.	J.F.
	29.		Brigade now transferred to Right Group under command of Lieut Colonel Duncan (255th Bde).	J.F.
			Day firing carried out on Targets 9A and 6.	
			Night firing as before. Special bursts at 10.15 p.m. 11.30 p.m. and 1.30 A.M.	J.F.
	30.		Registration carried out by Batteries.	J.F.
			Lieut Jordine and 2/Lt Adam proceeded on 10 days' leave	
			General Hafield held conference of Brigade Commanders at 260th Brigade Headquarters	J.F.
			C/260 Battery transferred to Left Group (Lt. Colonel Bryan).	J.F.

Thomas Chisholm Lieut
for Major
Comdg. 260th (Howitzer) Bde. R.F.A.

CONFIDENTIAL.
No. 21(A)
HIGHLAND
DIVISION.

Vol 15

Confidential

WAR DIARY
of
260th (LOWLAND) BRIGADE R.F.A.

From 1st December 1916
to 31 December 1916

WAR DIARY or INTELLIGENCE SUMMARY

Army Form C. 2118.

Place	Date 1916 Dec.	Hour	Summary of Events and Information	Remarks and references to Appendices
The Field	1		Bombardment of enemy trenches and communications behind lines by all batteries from 11.30 to 12 noon with pauses. Rate of fire 4 rounds per gun per minute.	
	2.		Night firing by 18 Pdr. Batteries on targets 6 & 9A (100 rounds per Battery) Lieut. Williams R.A.M.C. proceeded on 10 days leave - Capt. Titmas took over duties of m.o.	
	3		Night firing by 18 Pdr. batteries. General Oldfield visited Battery positions.	
	4.		Lieut. H.S. Cardwell reported for duty. Posted meantime to D Battery. Fatigue party of 60 men from 8th Royal Scots and T.M. Battery reported for work on new Group H.Q. 2/Lieut. Dick and Jackson laid wire to front line. 2/Lt. Dick remaining as F.O.O.	
	5.		General Harper and General Oldfield visited Battery positions. Captain A.G. Simpson proceeded to England in relief of officer exchanged. Lieut. Colonel Oldham returned from leave and resumed command of Brigade. Lieut. Colonel Alpham assumed command of Right Group. Night firing by all 18 Pdr. Batteries on Group on targets 7, 16, 9, 10, 22. 100 rounds per battery.	
	6.		Major Parker and Lieut. D.J.C. Kerswith proceeded on 10 days leave. Day misty - observation impossible. Night firing by 18 pdr. Batteries on targets 1, 17, A1, 15, 20. 100 rounds per Battery.	

Army Form C. 2118.

WAR DIARY
or
INTELLIGENCE SUMMARY
(Erase heading not required.)

Instructions regarding War Diaries and Intelligence Summaries are contained in F. S. Regs., Part II. and the Staff Manual respectively. Title Pages will be prepared in manuscript.

Place	Date	Hour	Summary of Events and Information	Remarks and references to Appendices
The field	1916 Dec. 8.		Ordinary day firing. Any night.	
			Night firing on Targets 3, 9, 40, 6, 11	
	9.		Day misty	
			Night firing on Targets 7, 15, 2, 22, 19	
	10.		Day clear. Registration carried out by Batteries.	
			Grand grunt trench registered by Howitzers.	
			Night firing on Targets 1, 9, 17, 6, 12.	
			A/260 Battery. One man killed and two wounded with 3 horses bringing up ammunition.	
	11.		Day fine. Observation good. Enemy movement fired on.	
			Night firing on Targets 1, 16, 10, 22, 1.	
	12.		2/Lieut Cardwell sent to Hospital.	
			Day firing on enemy movement and roads and approaches.	
			Retaliation asked for by Infantry for shelling of front line trenches.	
			Night firing on Targets 7, 42, 17, 13, 28.	
	13.		Registration and Bursts of fire carried out.	
		4.15 p.m.	Burst of fire at 4.15 p.m. on gun position at G.32 c 5.2.	
		6.30 & 9. p.m.	Read from R.5.d 80 to R.5.d 0.8 was barraged by six 18 pdrs. firing 1 round per gun per minute.	
			Night firing by Howitzers.	

WAR DIARY
or
INTELLIGENCE SUMMARY

Army Form C. 2118.

Place	Date 1916 Dec	Hour	Summary of Events and Information	Remarks and references to Appendices
The Field	14.		Registration and enemy movement fired on. Night firing on targets 16, 4, 12, 15, 39. 100 rounds per 18 pdr. battery – Howitzers on Trench Junctions and communications.	
	15.	8.30 AM	Lieuts Harvey and Graham proceeded on 10 days leave. Burst of fire on Battery position in L30b 3 rounds per gun per minute for two minutes. Night firing on special targets.	
	16.		Registration and General firing carried out. Special engagement of Hostile Battery Positions by all batteries in Group. Night firing on special targets.	
	17.	3.0 pm	Movement fire on enemy Roads and Trenches carried out. Hostile Battery position engaged by all batteries. Night firing on special Targets. 2/Lieut Loick wounded by direct hit on O.P.	
	18.		Bursts of motored fire carried out. Special bombardment of enemy dumps. Night firing on special targets. Captain McDougall RAMC reported to relieve Captain Kilner proceeding on leave.	
	19.		Lieut J.	

WAR DIARY or INTELLIGENCE SUMMARY

Army Form C. 2118.

Place	Date	Hour	Summary of Events and Information	Remarks and references to Appendices
Hofield.	1916 Dec. 19		Lieut Robertson and 2/Lieut Bruce sent to Hospital.	
			Ordinary day firing carried out.	
	20.		Special bombardment of dumps by all batteries.	
			Night firing on special targets.	
			Ordinary harassing firing carried out.	
			Special bombardment of enemy dumps.	
			Night firing on special targets.	
			Lieut Killaw returned from 10 days leave.	
			2/Lieut Macaulay sent to Hospital.	
	21.		Lieut Paulin and 2/Lieut Thomson proceeded on 10 days leave.	
			Bombardment of enemy dumps and Battery position in conjunction with Heavy Artillery.	
			Night firing on prearranged targets.	
	22.		2/Lieut Sinclair T.M. Battery reported for duty.	
			2/Lieut Hay " " " "	
			Enemy Battery positions and dumps bombarded in conjunction with Heavy Artillery.	
			Night firing as before.	
	23.		2/Lieut Wigg went to Hospital.	
			Enemy dumps fired on	
			Night firing as before.	

WAR DIARY
or
INTELLIGENCE SUMMARY.

Army Form C. 2118.

(Erase heading not required.)

Place	Date 1916 Dec.	Hour	Summary of Events and Information	Remarks and references to Appendices
The Field	24		Lieut. Nesmith returned from leave.	Yes
			2/Lieut Cardwell returned from Hospital.	Yes
			Lieut. Colonel Oldham went to Divisional Artillery.	Yes
			Ordinary day and night firing carried out.	Yes
	25	10.7AM	Rocket signal test by Infantry carried out. – Satisfactory.	Yes
			Salvoes were fired at 8 A.M. 12 noon 5 p.m. and 5.5 p.m. by any gun in Fifth Army.	Yes
			Night firing as before.	Yes
	26		Unobserved fire on enemy communications and trenches.	Yes
			Night firing as usual.	Yes
	27		2/Lieut M.D. Alderson reported for duty with D.A.C. Attached to 2/Sec Battery.	Yes
			Bursts of fire on enemy trenches &c throughout day.	Yes
			Night firing as usual.	Yes
	28		Lieut. H.H. Harvey reported from leave.	Yes
			Lieut. C.H.C. Prentice proceeded on 10 days' leave	Yes
			2/Lieut. H.G. Lockhart reported for duty from D.A.C.	Yes
			Bursts of fire carried out and registrations checked.	Yes
			Night firing as usual.	Yes

Army Form C. 2118.

WAR DIARY
or
INTELLIGENCE SUMMARY.

(Erase heading not required.)

Instructions regarding War Diaries and Intelligence Summaries are contained in F. S. Regs., Part II. and the Staff Manual respectively. Title pages will be prepared in manuscript.

Place	Date	Hour	Summary of Events and Information	Remarks and references to Appendices
In Field.	1916 Dec. 29.		Lieut W.B. Graham reported from leave.	
			Burst of fire as before.	
			Night firing as before.	
			B/260 Battery employed in taking up new position alongside "A" Battery.	
	30.		B/260 removed 2 guns to position alongside "A" Battery.	
			Batteries engaged draining positions after heavy rain.	
			Night firing as usual.	
	31.		Work on battery positions continued.	
			Night firing as before.	

Malcolm[?] Lieut Colonel
Comdg. 260 (Northern) Brigade R.F.A.

Vol 16

CONFIDENTIAL
No 21(?)
HIGHLAND
DIVISION.

C O N F I D E N T I A L

W A R   D I A R Y

OF

260th (LOWLAND) BRIGADE, R. F. A.

From 1st January 1917 to 31st January 1917.

Army Form C. 2118.

CONFIDENTIAL
No 21(A)
HIGHLAND DIVISION.

WAR DIARY
or
INTELLIGENCE SUMMARY.
(Erase heading not required.)

Place	Date 1917	Hour	Summary of Events and Information	Remarks and references to Appendices
The released	Jan 1.		Lieut. S. Thurrock proceeded on 10 days leave.	J.R.
	2/3		Situation normal.	J.R.
	3.		Lieut. Anderson, 34th Brigade came to take over telephone lines etc.	J.R.
	4.		Right Group handed over to 2nd Division. Headquarters moved to Wagon Lines at Bouquemaison.	J.R.
	5.		Brigade marched to Amplier.	J.R.
	6.		Brigade marched to MEZEROLLES. 2 Batteries "A" & "B". – D to OCCOCHES – A battery temporarily attached to 255 Brigade. Proceeded to Fegincourt for billets.	J.R.
	7.		The Brigade marched to BEALCOURT. "A" battery rejoined.	J.R.
	8.		The Brigade marched to CADOURS.	J.R.
	9.			
	10.		Batteries employed clearing up generally and going into new horse lines.	J.R.
	12.		Intimation first received that Brigade was to be broken up, the various Batteries being distributed among various Divisions	J.R.
	13.		Lieut. S. Thurrock reported from 10 days leave.	J.R.

WAR DIARY
or
INTELLIGENCE SUMMARY.
(Erase heading not required.)

Army Form C. 2118.

Place	Date	Hour	Summary of Events and Information	Remarks and references to Appendices
The Fleet	1917 Jan 16		2/Lieut Baleman proceeded on 10 days leave.	L.F.
	22.		Lieut. Wishart and Lieut Hall proceed on 10 days leave.	L.F.
	23.		2/Lieut J. Hamilton posted to B/260.	
			2/Lieut W.E. Macnay posted to A/260.	
			2/Lieut T. Hall posted to A/260.	
			Lieut. G.E. Hutchison attached to B/260 for duty.	L.F.
			2/Lieut G.E. Hutchison attached to B/260 for duty.	
	25.		Right and Left sections of C/260 battery proceeded to join 255 and 256 Brigades respectively.	
			Capt F.J. Bonner posted to D/255.	L.F.
			Lieut W.R. Graham posted to D/256.	L.F.
	28.		2/Lieut. G.E. Hutchison (late C. Battery) posted to 517 T.M. Battery.	L.F.
	30.		2/Lieut Baleman returned from 10 days leave.	
	31.		10th to 31st. Programme of Instruction. drill. recreational training etc carried out from day to day by batteries in accordance with instructions.	

Norman Smith
for Lieut Colonel
Commanding 260 (Central) S Bde

Vol 17

Confidential

WAR DIARY

of

260 (LOWLAND) BRIGADE, R.F.A.

From 1st February 1917
To 28th February 1917.
both inclusive

Army Form C. 2118.

WAR DIARY
or
INTELLIGENCE SUMMARY.
(Erase heading not required.)

Instructions regarding War Diaries and Intelligence Summaries are contained in F.S. Regs., Part II. and the Staff Manual respectively. Title pages will be prepared in manuscript.

Place	Date 1917 February	Hour	Summary of Events and Information	Remarks and references to Appendices
In field	1.		2/Lieut. B.A. SALVESEN relinquishes the post of Staff Officer on posting to B/260 Battery.	
	4.		Lieut. H.B. CARDWELL A/260 Battery appointed Orderly Officer vice 2/Lieut. G.A. Salvesen. Lieut. J.R. WISHART returned from 10 days leave. Lieut. T. HALL " " "	
	5.		Brigade disbanded, A/260 becoming C/315 Brigade attached 63rd Division. B/260 " C/86 " " 19th " C/260 " D/84 " " 18th "	
			Headquarters 260 F. Brigade marched to NOYELLE-EN-CHAUSSEE. Batteries being left at CAOURS.	
	6.		Brigade Headquarters marched to BOUBERS-SUR-CANCHE.	
	7.		Brigade Headquarters marched to HERNICOURT.	
	8.		Brigade Headquarters marched to HOUVELIN.	
	19.		Brigade Headquarters marched to OURTON.	
	28.		Lieut. Colonel F.T. OLDHAM, Lieut. R.T. STURROCK and R.S.M. O. ROGERS left for England to take over new Brigade at WOOLWICH. Headquarters remaining meantime at OURTON under Lieut CARDWELL.	

[signature]
Lieut
for Lieut Colonel
Comdg. 260 (Rowland) Brigade R.F.A.

www.ingramcontent.com/pod-product-compliance
Lightning Source LLC
Chambersburg PA
CBHW081450160426
43193CB00013B/2433